Original title:
Apples and Adventure

Copyright © 2025 Creative Arts Management OÜ
All rights reserved.

Author: Ryan Sterling
ISBN HARDBACK: 978-1-80586-288-8
ISBN PAPERBACK: 978-1-80586-760-9

The Rogue's Orchard Road

In a grove where fruits do giggle,
A rogue set off with a jolly wiggle.
He tiptoed 'neath the laughing trees,
And danced with shadows in the breeze.

With a basket slightly askew,
He chased a fruit that brightly flew.
It rolled away with a cheeky smirk,
As he let out a squeal and a perk.

Through the branches, he took a leap,
To grab the fruit that refused to keep.
It dodged and darted, oh what a tease,
While he landed squarely atop some bees!

His friends nearby could barely stand,
As he flailed around like a marching band.
With laughter ringing loud and clear,
They joined the dance, no hint of fear.

So if you find a rogue in flight,
Just know he's chasing fruits of light.
Join the fun, it's quite the show,
In the orchard where giggles flow!

Chasing the Windfall

In a field wet with morning dew,
A rogue fruit fell, a sudden coup.
We sprinted fast, we laughed out loud,
To catch the prize, oh, so proud.

A dog zoomed past, a squirrel too,
All for that snack, our laughter grew.
We tumbled down, a perfect spill,
Who knew chasing fruit could thrill?

Blossoms Beyond the Horizon

Petals dancing in the breeze,
We chased a dream, with such great ease.
A cartwheeled hat, a pie on the run,
Our laughter echoed, what perfect fun!

We climbed the trees, we swung and twirled,
In a world of sweetness, we swirled.
With sticky hands and grins so wide,
We raced the sun, our joy our guide.

The Fruitful Odyssey

Through forests thick and hills so steep,
We found a stash, oh, what a heap!
With every bite, a laugh we'd share,
As friends united, without a care.

A critter stole our final prize,
We chased it down, oh, such surprise!
In a merry chase, we lost track of time,
Chasing treasures, all things sublime.

Nightfall in the Grove

As shadows danced, we gathered near,
A glow of lights, the laughter here.
With stories spun of wild delight,
Each bounce and joke brought pure delight.

The moon above, our eager host,
We toasted snacks, our midnight boast.
With crumbs and giggles all around,
In the grove, true joy was found.

Breezes in the Orchard's Heart

In the orchard where the laughter flows,
Chasing critters, tripping on toes.
Squirrels giggle, tossing their treats,
As we race past, oh what feats!

Breezes dance, the branches sway,
We leap through shadows, come what may.
Giggles echo, the sun shines bright,
In this garden of pure delight.

Journeys Through Crimson Canopies

With baskets slung, we hit the trail,
Dodging bees and a barking whale.
A treasure hunt in every bush,
As we run with a joyful rush.

Crimson crowns atop our heads,
As we dodge low flying breads.
A silly dance, a wild spin,
Under canopies where laughter begins.

Tangled Trails of the Mind

Winding paths through thoughts a-twist,
Finding giggles we can't resist.
A juggle here, a tumble there,
In a maze of fun, we declare.

Ideas bounce like springy balls,
As we navigate the orchard walls.
Maps that lead us to the chime,
Of laughter echoing through our time.

A Fruitful Quest

In search of treats, we plot and scheme,
With dreams so wild, it's all a dream!
A pirate's hunt for treasure fair,
With giggles stuck in falling hair.

Through grassy fields and trees so tall,
We carry hopes, we might just fall.
But every slip brings a new jest,
On this whimsical, quirky quest.

Echoes of the Orchard

In a grove where trees wear hats,
Squirrels hold wild acrobat chats.
The fruit tries to roll away,
While the sun starts its playful sway.

Bees buzz in a goofy dance,
Whispers of mischief, not a chance.
A wooden sign wobbles and creaks,
"Pick me first!" the old tree squeaks.

Rabbits hop in a jumpy tune,
Dodging shadows of a sneaky raccoon.
A picnic blanket starts to fly,
As the wind lets out a cheeky sigh.

Laughter echoes, the day is bright,
In this orchard, everything feels right.
The moon peeks in, a curious mate,
And a gnome giggles at his plate.

The Enigmatic Grove

Beneath the branches, secrets hide,
With giggles from the squirrels that glide.
A jester tree tickles the skies,
While butterflies gossip, oh so sly.

A dancing worm wears a tiny crown,
Prancing about, refusing to frown.
The groundhogs debate the best snack,
Who can munch faster? No one holds back!

The shadows stretch with silly grace,
As a hedgehog trips in a comical race.
The apples wink, their cheeks all aglow,
Each thud and tumble puts on a show.

A frog jumps in for a dramatic dive,
Splashing the crickets—oh, they strive!
In this grove of whimsical delight,
Every turn brings a fun surprise bright.

The Path of the Glimmering Orchard

On a road lined with shiny globes,
Crickets wear little jeweled robes.
A path of glimmer, twists and twirls,
Where every step jostles and whirls.

A monkey swings from branch to branch,
Chasing after an unplanned chance.
Each fruit sings a tune of cheer,
As the breeze carries laughter near.

With every stomp, the ground erupts,
Frogs leap out, with squishy thuds.
An old tree shakes with a joyful quiver,
Making all who pass stop and shiver.

The sun does a jig, the clouds a spin,
A picnic table suddenly grins.
On this path, part mirth, part glee,
No one can resist the playful spree.

Dreamscapes of the Orchard

In dreamland, where the harvest beams,
The trees sprout twinkling starry dreams.
A giggling gnome with a silly hat,
Claims he's king of this playful habitat.

The grass tickles toes, a zoetrope spin,
As shadows play tag beneath the skin.
A plump pear recites a knock-knock joke,
While laughter erupts in a friendly poke.

Fruit flies wear monocles, look quite smart,
While wise old owls tell tales off the chart.
"Once upon a time," they always start,
"Adventures sprout time after time, heart!"

In this whimsical land, time takes flight,
With dreams that twirl like kites in the night.
Beneath the stars, with a laugh and a chime,
The orchard's secrets unfold in rhyme.

Beneath the Canopy of Dreams

Under trees with fruits so bright,
We climbed so high, oh what a sight!
Bobbing heads like apples on a spree,
Who knew that laughter would set us free?

Silly faces and kinfolk near,
We danced with joy and held no fear.
A swinging ride on a bough so wide,
We laughed as we slipped, side by side.

With juice in hand, we felt so bold,
Every secret tale we told.
The shadows played with a gentle tease,
As we nibbled fruits, our minds at ease.

Taste of the Wanderer

With a tickle of zest beneath my nose,
I journeyed far where the wild winds blow.
A map made of laughter, a compass of cheer,
I chuckled aloud, 'This place feels clear!'

Through fields of green and skies of blue,
I stumbled upon a crew so new.
We shared a taste of the sweetest treat,
With giggles erupting from every seat.

The fruit we found made our trip grand,
In a wobbly cart, we made our stand.
Twists and turns led us on this bliss,
Who knew that wandering felt like this?

The Lemonade of Life's Adventures

In a world with twists and silly bends,
We made fresh drinks and called them friends.
With laughter bubbling like fizzy waves,
We toasted to life, the bold and brave.

Each sip a giggle, a frothy delight,
Chasing shadows till the sun took flight.
Lemonade rivers where we did glide,
With splashes of joy and a fruity ride.

Moments like this are treasures so rare,
Every chuckle showed we didn't care.
We danced to tunes of the buzzing bees,
In a syrupy world where we did seize.

Pies and Paths Untraveled

On a trail of crumbles, we found our fun,
Chasing wild dreams as the day was done.
With pie in hand and laughter so wide,
In every bite, adventures did guide.

We stumbled upon a bakery's delight,
With scents of cinnamon, it felt just right.
Each slice a story of a life well-spent,
With crumbs like confetti, a feast so bent.

As paths entwined in a sugary haze,
We skipped through moments of vibrant days.
With every laugh, each silly grin,
Life served us smiles with a generous spin.

Green Canopy Chronicles

Underneath the leafy crowns,
A critter sneezes, tumbles down.
With a wink, he shakes his head,
"I thought this was my cozy bed!"

Swinging vines and spinning leaves,
Tangled tales that nature weaves.
A squirrel on a daring quest,
To find a nut—his favorite guest.

The birds are chirping, full of cheer,
They join the dance, they all appear.
One trip, a flip, a twirl, a glide,
Together they all take the ride.

In the end they find a snack,
A juicy treat—no looking back.
With laughter echoing through the trees,
Who knew fun came with the breeze?

Fables of the Forgotten Grove

In a grove where shadows play,
Silly secrets drift away.
A turtle racing with the sun,
Who's the winner? Just for fun!

A rabbit hops, he's feeling spry,
With candy dreams that float on high.
He trips and flips, the world goes round,
Giggles rise up from the ground.

A fox in boots joins in the chase,
With flair and charm, he sets the pace.
He trips on roots, oh what a sight,
The laughter echoes, pure delight.

In this place of whimsy and cheer,
Joyful spirits always near.
With mirth and glee, they sing their prose,
Where funny fables bloom and grow.

Nature's Poetic Journey

Through the fields, they trot along,
With merry hearts and silly song.
A breeze tickles, leaves do sway,
Chasing dreams, they shout hooray!

A ladybug dons shades of red,
Sipping nectar, feeling fed.
She waves to flies in frantic flight,
While ants rally for the night.

With giggles caught among the trees,
A picnic spills with dandelion breeze.
Sandwiches take flight, they soar,
Nature laughing, wanting more.

So hold your apple, take a bite,
Share the laughter under starlight.
For every chuckle, every cheer,
Nature's joy is always near.

The Harvest of New Horizons

Beneath the sky, two friends set sail,
On a leaf boat, with humor trail.
They paddle hard, they splash and play,
Who knew bliss was just a sway?

With berries bouncing, oh so sweet,
They can't decide what's best to eat.
One feisty berry starts to roll,
And begins a journey toward their goal.

The laughter swells, they race the sun,
With every stumble, more fun begun.
Each fruit they land, a tasty prize,
Life's little moments, the best surprise.

From sunset skies to morning dew,
The world awaits, for me and you.
For joy combined with every bite,
Shall keep our hearts forever light.

Beneath the Boughs of Wonder

In a tree where giggles soar,
A squirrel spins tales of yore.
Beneath the boughs, we laugh and play,
As fruits of mystery lead the way.

With a quest for treasures sweet,
Down the path, we skip our feet.
Each bite brings unexpected glee,
As we munch beneath the leafy spree.

A bug with boots joins our parade,
He waltzes through the orchard shade.
We chase him round, we tumble and twirl,
In this sweet world, where dreams unfurl.

Discovery waits with a cheeky grin,
As we take turns to spin and spin.
In the end, our laughter grows,
Beneath the boughs, where wonder glows.

A Palette of Orchard Dreams

In a field of colors bright,
We splash around, what a sight!
With every munch and playful shout,
There's magic, fun, and no doubt.

The ground is soft, a bouncy bed,
Where worries vanish, and joy is spread.
Each fruit we find, a vibrant prize,
With painted smiles and glowing eyes.

A critter dressed in dapper wear,
Tells us tales of fruits that dare.
Sweet juices spill, we laugh with glee,
What a world for you and me!

As sunset paints the sky in hues,
We gather whispers of the blues.
Adventure calls, come join the dance,
In a palette of dreams, let's take a chance.

The Fruit of Curiosity

Curious critters round the bend,
Exploring paths that never end.
With every step, a surprise to find,
Each zesty nibble, a treat for the mind.

A taste of mischief in every bite,
We giggle and run, hearts feeling light.
Join the race, let silliness rule,
In a garden where wonder is the fuel.

A wobbly rabbit joins in the fun,
With floppy ears, he's on the run.
We share our snacks, the flavors blend,
As laughter echoes, the day won't end.

The sweetest fruits hang in the air,
We toss them high, without a care.
Delightfully silly, we leap and cheer,
In the fruit of curiosity, joy is near.

Whimsical Paths in the Greenery

On whimsical paths where dreams collide,
We bounce along, side by side.
With every twist, a riddle to solve,
This cheerful place makes hearts evolve.

In the tangle of vines, we spin and sway,
Wishing for our merry play.
A fruit-bearer with a hat too tall,
Shares secret maps that delight us all.

Mirthful critters dance with style,
As we trample through the greenery a while.
With giggles light and joyful zest,
In this adventure, we are truly blessed.

At twilight's close, the stars will beam,
We'll wake again, to chase our dream.
With a wink, we whisper, "What's next in store?"
On whimsical paths, we'll explore once more.

The Orchard's Secret Map

In a grove where shadows linger,
There's a treasure map with a twinkle.
X marks the spot under the tree,
Where giggles grow like fruit so free.

A squirrel wears glasses, oh what a sight,
Chasing his dreams till the fall of night.
He scurries and schemes with nimble grace,
Planting jokes in that secret place.

Each apple burst with laughter loud,
Like little fireworks, they make us proud.
The wind whispers secrets in a playful chat,
While bees in top hats do a ballerina spat.

So we gather round, the fun's just begun,
With silly songs, we dance and run.
In the orchard, joy is a merry affair,
With dreams and giggles filling the air.

Harvesting Dreams

With baskets in hand like curious thieves,
We search for dreams hanging on leaves.
Each one glowing, a burst of cheer,
We pluck them softly, giggling near.

The sun shines brightly, a mischievous sprite,
While butterflies join the laugh-so-bright.
We stumble and trip in our wild, bold quest,
But every laugh leads to joy's biggest fest.

Oh, the strange fruit with faces so wide,
Some wink at us, others can't hide.
Mischief flows like juice in the air,
As silly puns sprout everywhere.

We fill our baskets with joy and surprise,
Each fruit a twist in our playful guise.
In this orchard of dreams, we're never too old,
For laughter and love, they're worth more than gold.

The Trail of Twisted Roots

Down a path where the trees do twist,
We wander with laughter, none can resist.
Roots that tangle, a fun little plight,
Step carefully, or you'll take an unexpected flight.

With each footfall, the giggles grow loud,
As we tease the branches, feeling so proud.
Jumping over roots with playful glee,
While squirrels cheer on from their tall tree.

A signpost points to the land of surprise,
"Beware of the fruit that steals your eyes!"
We tremble and laugh, but in jest, not fear,
For every strange fruit brings more fun near.

So we wander this path, hand in hand,
Chasing dreams through laugh and sand.
In the maze of roots, we've found our way,
A whimsical journey brightens our day.

The Fruitful Expedition

Off we go on a journey bright,
With curiosity as our guiding light.
The cart is creaky, full of delight,
As we sing silly songs in the soft sunlight.

A butterfly leads with a wink and flutter,
While we giggle at the sound of our own chatter.
Each twist and turn, a new joke we share,
Laughter erupts in the open air.

The fruits dance wildly upon their branch,
Inviting us all to a carefree prance.
Each one says, "Pick me, I'm ripe and fun!"
As we pile our treasures, we're not yet done.

So we laugh and we eat 'til the day is done,
With smiles so big that they shine like the sun.
In our fruitful quest, with joy all around,
We find that the laughter is the true golden crown.

A Journey in Crimson

In a basket stuck on a sunny day,
A round red fruit rolled far away.
It climbed a hill, then slipped and spun,
Chasing a squirrel just to have some fun.

A raccoon joined and they ran and played,
Through the bushes, they swiftly swayed.
But then a bee sang a silly tune,
And they danced under the light of the moon.

The Enchanted Grove

In a grove where giggles fill the air,
A round delight hung without a care.
It rolled with laughter, tumbled about,
While the leaves whispered secrets with a shout.

A rabbit hopped in with a little cart,
To collect the fruit, a quirky art.
But a mouse in a hat stole the show,
As they paraded in a row with a glow.

Tales of the Wandering Seeds

Oh, wandering seeds with a mind of play,
They dared to roll and whisk away.
Across the meadows, they danced and spun,
Chasing their dreams 'til the day was done.

A gentle breeze became their guide,
While dandelions giggled, standing beside.
They hitchhiked a ride on a passing bee,
Buzzing through laughter, wild and free.

Beneath the Canopy of Stars

Beneath the stars where critters scheme,
A plump delight rolled with a gleam.
It whispered wishes to the moon above,
Hoping to find a little love.

A constellation of friends came near,
Each sharing tales over laughter and cheer.
With starlit faces and a dance so bright,
They twirled till dawn, in pure delight.

Whispers of the Harvest Sun

In a grove where laughter grows,
Fruits of mischief dance in rows.
A squirrel plots his daring heist,
Grabbing snacks while friends have sliced.

Giddy giggles fill the air,
As wormy tales weave everywhere.
One cheeky bite, the fruit's surprise,
Amouthful of seeds, oh, what a prize!

Bouncing branches, a playful ride,
Chasing shadows far and wide.
A sticky hand, a starry grin,
Who knew that munching could begin?

Underneath the rustling trees,
Plans unfold like buzzing bees.
With every crunch, a joyful yell,
In the feast of fun, we dwell!

The Lost Orchard Expedition

We set sail on seas of green,
With plucky friends and a plan routine.
But the map we had was upside down,
We found a fruit stand in a clown town.

Mismatched socks and giggles echoed,
As we searched for the treasure that glowed.
An old man said, 'Look high, look low!'
But we tripped over each other in the show.

A dog with a hat joined our quest,
Claiming he knew the very best.
With a wag and a woof, he led the way,
To a shimmering orchard where we could play.

We filled our bags and danced with glee,
As shadows stretched beneath the trees.
Lost our way but found our fun,
Who needs a map when you've got sun?

Cinnamon Trails and Sweet Surprises

A sprinkle of spice in the warm air,
Greeted by giggles, we could only stare.
Sticky fingers and giggly sighs,
Where each twist and turn reveals a prize.

With caramel rivers and nutty bends,
We raced together, oh, what fun it sends!
A river of fudge, a mountain of cheer,
Two thieves would steal what we all hold dear.

The scent of joy wafts in the breeze,
Sweet surprises among the trees.
With each treat that we devoured,
Our laughter blossomed, forever empowered.

Cinnamon trails, a merry chase,
With jolly cheers, we'd claim our place.
In this land of sweetness and cheer,
Let's savor the journey, year after year!

Enchanted Seedlings

In a garden where whimsy grows,
Little sprouts hide in funky clothes.
A beetle named Bob, with a twinkling eye,
Tried planting giggles instead of pie.

Wiggly worms wear party hats,
While butterflies dance in friendly spats.
Petunias plot their clever schemes,
As sunlight flutters in happy beams.

Come join the fun, the playful cheer,
In a world where seedlings disappear.
For every bloom unveils a quest,
With scents and sights that are simply the best.

A twist, a turn, a pop of glee,
In this enchanted patch, we decree:
Laughing blossoms and silly scenes,
A garden of joy, bursting at the seams!

Voices of the Boughs

Up high the boughs do sway,
With chatter that can't decay,
The tales of fruit that have been,
And secrets nestled in between.

The squirrels plot a heist so sly,
While birds in chorus flutter by,
Each rustle brings a chuckle loud,
As nature dances, proud and cowed.

We giggle at the bees that buzz,
In trousers made of nectar fuzz,
They wear their stripes with such great flair,
While pollen fights pickpocket air.

So join the laughter, have some fun,
In orchards where our hearts do run,
With voices of the boughs in tune,
We'll sing beneath the talking moon.

Fables from the Fruit Trail

In the shade where shadows blend,
Lies a path with tales to send,
Of wily crabs and slippery fish,
Who grant the wildest dreams to wish.

A rabbit dons a tiny cape,
Declaring he'll escape his fate,
While wise old owls hoot in glee,
And giggle at the daily spree.

The grapes all whisper juicy lies,
Claiming sunsets fill the skies,
And when picked, will sing a tune,
That'll charm the stars and moon.

So wander down this fruity course,
Where laughter flows, a joyous force,
Each fable shared, a silly jest,
Amongst the trees, we are the best.

The Twilit Orchard Quest

When twilight graces leafy hue,
A quest begins for me and you,
With lanterns made from glowing fruit,
And giggles dancing in pursuit.

The raccoons join the merry chase,
With sticky hands but happy face,
Chasing shadows, making noise,
Each step a wonder, full of joys.

A mischief of the tomcat near,
Pretends to prowl, but holds dear
The jars of jam we've left behind,
As we unleash our playful mind.

So through the orchard, let us roam,
With laughter echoing our home,
In search of treasures bright and sweet,
On this bizarre and fun-filled beat.

Adventures in the Shade of Blossoms

Under boughs with blossoms white,
We craft our plans, our hearts ignite,
With a map drawn on a crinkled leaf,
To find a world beyond belief.

The sneaky worms, they roll and twirl,
While ladybugs around us whirl,
Each petal whispers secrets grand,
Of where we wander, hand in hand.

The honey's sticky but so divine,
We dab it on like it's a sign,
"Find the golden treasure small!"
With laughter echoing through it all.

So mingle in this fragrant air,
With every prank, we're light as air,
For in this fun beneath the blooms,
Our laughter fills the crowded rooms.

The Quest for Forbidden Fruit

In a land where cravings sprout,
A rogue with pockets turned inside out.
He climbed a tree with a laugh and a shout,
For the juicy prize that made him a lout.

He slipped on a branch, took a tumble with flair,
Landing in dirt with leaves in his hair.
The fruit rained down like a sweet, sticky fair,
While squirrels laughed loud, no hint of despair.

With sticky fingers and a grin oh so wide,
He challenged the squirrels, "Come take a ride!"
But they all just chittered, "You silly old guide,
We're the kings of this grove, with nothing to hide!"

So he picked up a fruit, with a wink and a tease,
"If you think you're the best, try this one, if you please!"
But the moment he bit, he fell to his knees,
For the taste was so sour, it brought him to wheeze!

Cascading Orchard Dreams

Through fields where laughter echoes and rolls,
A treasure hunt for shimmer and souls.
They bounced on hills like a bunch of fools,
Collecting sweet gems, breaking all rules.

With baskets swinging, they marched with great glee,
Finding a spot with the biggest old tree.
One lad swung high, yelled, "Look at me!"
But he miscalculated, oh what a spree!

Down came the fruit like a carnival show,
Plopping on heads with a thump and a glow.
The giggles erupted, a wild tableau,
As fresh, fruity splats began their sweet flow.

They rolled on the ground, covered in luck,
In the orchard's embrace, they were never stuck.
With hearts full of joy and a touch of muck,
They vowed every fall tasted just like a pluck!

Wanderlust in the Grove

There once was a lad with a curious nose,
He dreamed of the wonders wherever he goes.
With pockets of snacks and a hat full of prose,
He ventured through pathways where nobody knows.

In the lush greens, he found a surprise,
A talking tree, with big, sleepy eyes.
It whispered, "Come closer, and take to the skies,
The fruit here is magic, no need for a prize."

He shook his head, what a silly old blunder,
But curiosity sparked like the crack of a thunder.
With each little bite, he felt light as a plunder,
Until he was floating—oh what a wonder!

He drifted on high, heard the giggles below,
As the ground shared its stories, all wild in a row.
The fruit was a trickster, the tree knew the show,
Turning wanderlust dreams into laughter's glow!

A Slice of Serendipity

In a small quirky market, where all things collide,
A fellow found fruits in a wild, fun ride.
He grabbed without thinking, not caring to decide,
And oh what a taste, like a car on a slide!

Each bite brought laughter, a tickle to share,
While friends clutched their bellies, gasping for air.
With flavors so wacky, like a unicorn's flare,
They danced with delight, not a single care.

Then came the great challenge, a brave little friend,
"I'll juggle these gems, just watch me ascend!"
But with a slip and a splash, it came to an end,
As fruits started flying, what fun they did send.

They donned fruity crowns, like kings of the scene,
With rinds for their scepters, all laughing obscene.
A slice of serendipity glowed in between,
Turning simple moments into a grand cuisine!

Secrets of the Orchard Traveler

In the orchard where giggles collide,
A traveler slips, takes a rather wild slide,
Bananas on branches, the map shows a plot,
But the treasure's a pear? Oh, that's what I thought!

A squirrel in a hat steals a basket of cheer,
While a raccoon sings songs of sweet souvenirs,
Each tree holds a tale, each leaf is a prank,
Who knew that the sweet could grow so very rank?

With hops like a bunny, I leap with delight,
Chasing shadows and whispers, into the night,
A hidden cache laughs, I stumble and swing,
The custodian's yell — what a marvelous thing!

Collecting my bounty, I gather a crew,
A dance with a hedgehog, who knew he could do?
The orchard's a circus, so wild and so bright,
With secrets aplenty to share in the twilight.

The Path of Sweet Discoveries

A path with no map leads to jesters and fun,
I tread with my buddy—a tater named Bun,
Each step's a delight, taking bites full of gold,
But the ground is a trap! Watch the mud, oh so bold!

Squirrels give advice, dressed up like old kings,
While clouds overhead debate all sorts of things,
A twist of the wrist brings a slip and a fall,
And what lands on my head? Just a plump fruitball!

Gathered round laughter, we toast with a cheer,
For underneath branches, the fun's always near,
So many surprises from sunset till dawn,
Even found a shoe? Where did my sock go wrong?

A beanstalk appears—who left this here?
With friends on my side, oh, there's nothing to fear,
Together we'll romp through this zany disguise,
With giggles and tricks, and wide-open eyes.

The Cider's Hidden Tale

Once a bottle of froth with a wink and a grin,
Told tales of an orchard where mischief begins,
With hiccups and chuckles, the cider confessed,
That nobody's perfect—oh, ain't that the jest!

It spoke of a barrel that danced in the rain,
While critters performed, their songs were insane,
A fox in a tux made a toast by the tree,
To flavors and folly—come join in, be free!

But one day a rumor crawled out with the mist,
That barrels are reapers! My, is that a twist!
With mugs raised high, we debated the lore,
While the laughter that bubbled escaped through the door!

Cheers till the sunrise! We guffaw and we cheer,
For each apple's a story that's waiting right here,
So drink up, dear friend, let's make this a tale,
Of laughter and cider, we never can fail.

Echoes of the Wild Harvest

In woods where the wild pranks play peekaboo,
Echoes of laughter fly high, round and true,
Gathering harvest, oh what a surprise,
Who knew pies could dance under twinkling skies?

Lizards in top hats, and owls sporting ties,
Joined in the fun, with big, wide-open eyes,
A scavenger hunt leads to silly old games,
With acorns and giggles, let's manage our aims!

The harvest is ripe, not just fruit but delight,
With stunts gone awry, we embrace every blight,
As raccoons debate if they need a new pot,
And I simply wonder, is this all for naught?

Every nook tells a tale, so don't be a bore,
With whispers of joy, let's explore even more,
With mischief afoot and a chuckle to spare,
A celebration awaits, join if you dare!

A Picnic Under Starry Skies

Beneath the stars, we spread our feast,
With sandwiches piled, we couldn't fit least.
A squirrel darted, stole a bite,
We chased it down, what a silly sight!

A drink of juice, a splash and roar,
It drenched my friend, oh, what a chore!
He danced and shook, like rain on grass,
We laughed so hard, time flew past!

The moonlight shined on our picnic spread,
While ants marched in, filled with dread.
"Leave the crumbs, we shout with glee,"
"Sharing is fun, come join the spree!"

As fireflies blinked, we told tall tales,
Of mystical lands and sky-bound trails.
With every crunch, our giggles grew,
A feast for stars, a sky of dew!

Adventures Between the Trees

In tangled branches, we played our parts,
Inventing a game that tickles our hearts.
A swing made of ropes, we took a leap,
Falling to laughter, not the heap!

A treasure map drawn, by a crayon blue,
Led us to nowhere; the trees just grew.
"Let's dig for gold!" my sister exclaimed,
But found only dirt, our hopes untamed!

A crow cawed loud, interrupting our plot,
"Where's the treasure?" we all laughed a lot.
He stole our snacks with a mischievous grin,
The bandit bird, oh, let the fun begin!

We climbed so high, it felt like flight,
Telling secrets under the daylight.
In nature's arms, we knew no fears,
Just endless fun, and silly cheers!

The Fruitful Road Ahead

On a winding path, we strolled in glee,
With baskets in hand, we hopped with glee.
The sound of crunching echoed loud,
As we munched on snacks, feeling proud.

"Look! A garden!" my friend did say,
We dashed right in, not a minute to sway.
The veggies giggled; the fruits sang tunes,
We joined their chorus under the moons!

A rolling pumpkin, oh what a trick,
It made us stumble, we fell in a flick!
With twirling laughter, we whispered "whoops!"
The veggies chuckled, they joined our loops!

As dusk drew near, a rabbit appeared,
Did he steal dinner? Our hopes veered!
"Chase him!" we shouted, in playful delight,
The fruit of our labor, what a silly night!

The Gilded Way

Down the lane where laughter blooms,
We chased the sun and chased the glooms.
A golden apple, perched on a branch,
It called to us, a gleeful chance!

With giggles high, we hatched a scheme,
To reach that fruit, a wild dream!
One climbed up, then slipped with flair,
Fell in the bushes; what a hilarious affair!

The prize rolled off, into the stream,
Splashing water, burst our gleam.
"Let's build a bridge!" we shouted in cheer,
With sticks and stones, a plan unclear.

With efforts grand, we strung a line,
That glittered bright, but just for a time.
The apple danced, a cheeky tease,
In the end, a fruitless search, but joy like these!

Fables of the Harvest Moon

Beneath the harvest moon so bright,
Critters dance, a funny sight.
A squirrel wears a tiny hat,
While a raccoon sings, imagine that!

They chase their tails and roll in heaps,
Sharing tales while the apple tree weeps.
A deer with glasses reads a book,
While sneaky foxes giggle and look.

The owl hoots jokes that make them chuckle,
As fireflies glow in a giggly shuffle.
They toast with cider, laughter flows,
What strange things happen when the moon glows!

So gather round, let stories brew,
In the orchard where the wild things grew.
With every bite, a tale unwinds,
A funny harvest, a feast, who finds?

Enigmatic Tracks of the Grove

In a grove where shadows play,
Funny footprints lead the way.
Was that a bear, or just a fox?
With laughter bouncing off the rocks!

A parrot squawks some silly news,
As critters wear their funky shoes.
Rabbits hop with twirling flair,
While turtles pause, too slow to care.

A party forms by a fallen log,
With a dancing chipmunk and a groggy frog.
They tap their feet on leafy ground,
As acorns tumble all around.

So follow those tracks, embrace the fun,
In the grove, there's mischief for everyone.
With every step, you'll laugh and cheer,
Wondering what's waiting, oh dear!

The Longing for the Orchard's Heart

A teddy bear sat on a tree branch high,
Pondering fruit with a dreamy sigh.
"Maybe pears?" he scratched his chin,
But apples just giggled at his whim.

He whispered sweet nothings to each fruit,
"I'm longing for a juicy hoot!"
Peaches blushed, plums turned around,
While the apples rolled, a funny sound.

So he climbed down with a wobbly leap,
To find the prize made for laughs, not sleep.
A pie was waiting, oh what a treat!
But it vanished quick with a chuckle and squeak.

Now teddy sits with a band of friends,
Where silly stories laugh and blend.
For in that heart of greens and gold,
Are memories made that never grow old!

Joys of the Juicy Venture

With basket in hand, a crew sets sail,
Across the field, through woods they trail.
A pineapple tries to join the game,
But dressed as a pirate, it's feeling lame!

They hop over streams, giggles abound,
Each jump a splash, laughter resounds.
An orange rolls down the grassy hill,
Chasing its dreams with a daring thrill.

A party of fruits, it's quite the sight,
Bananas sport shades, feeling quite right.
They sing on the path, in rhythm and cheer,
Spreading joy with each funny sneer.

Together they dance, through sun and shade,
Creating memories, together they're made.
Every ripe moment a juicy delight,
On this frolicking venture, everything's bright!

Captured by the Canopy

A tree with branches wide and tall,
I climbed up high, but almost fell.
With fruit like jewels, glowing bright,
I shared my snack with a passing kite.

The leaves they rustled, giggles soared,
As squirrels debated, who got the hoard.
I swayed and swung, what a crazy ride,
With juice on my chin, I felt so spry.

Beneath the sun, my laughter rang,
While bees buzzed sweetly, a silly clang.
My friends all gathered, a merry crew,
As we tossed the fruit like unripe goo.

In a whirlwind of fun, we danced about,
Chasing our shadows, filled with shouts.
Captured by laughter, lost in the leaves,
Our tales would grow like harvests from trees.

The Legend of the Sweet Harvest

In a quirky town where stories bloom,
A legend started in a farmer's room.
With tales of fruit that shined so gold,
And mischief-making, brash and bold.

It spoke of a pie so rich, divine,
Made from treasures beneath the vine.
But first you'd have to dodge a cat,
Who loved fresh treats and liked to chat.

One day we schemed a plan so grand,
With a basket ready and a bold band.
But as we picked, we heard a yell,
The farmer's dog rang a warning bell!

We raced and scurried, dodging nips,
With laughter bursting from our lips.
Legend grew as we fled the scene,
Leaving behind a sweet, sticky sheen.

A Symphony of Ripe Senses

Under a sky, a radiant blue,
We gathered together, a curious crew.
With baskets ready, hearts full of cheer,
The fruits began calling, come hither, my dear!

The colors danced, so vibrant, so loud,
As we tiptoed through nature, feeling so proud.
There were reds and greens, each more bizarre,
The squirrels were jamming, a nutty rock star!

One misstep led to an orchard's spree,
We slipped and we slid, oh how we did flee!
Squashed underfoot, the squishy delight,
Turned our escapade into a slippery sight.

Senses ablaze, we hooted and cheered,
As juice ran down, we laughed, never feared.
A symphony played through laughter and squish,
Of sweet, silly moments, oh what a dish!

Spontaneous Adventures Amongst the Boughs

One sunny day, we jumped with glee,
"Let's climb those branches, just you and me!"
We scaled the heights, our spirits so free,
While birds overhead sang in harmony.

The fruits hung tempting, like treasures to find,
With daring and laughter, we didn't mind.
One friend slipped, in a most graceful way,
A tumble, a roll, and "Please save my day!"

But back to the chase went our merry band,
With sticky fingers and fruit still in hand.
Giggles erupted with every small fall,
Spontaneous moments, we cherished them all.

As daylight faded, we made our way down,
A feast of sweet chaos, this wild little town.
With tales of our antics to share and delight,
We promised more adventures, under the moonlight.

The Boughs That Call Us

In the orchard, laughter plays,
Chasing shadows, sunny rays.
A twist, a turn, a hidden path,
Whispers echo, sparking math.

Branches sway and wiggle free,
What a sight for you and me!
A rogue fruit lands upon my head,
Oops, I think I'm seeing red!

Down the lane, the fruit parade,
Sticky fingers, a grand charade.
Fruits in pockets, giggles burst,
A wild party, oh, how we thirst!

In this realm of green delight,
Each bite brings a silly fight.
Caught in glee, we dance and sway,
Adventures bloom in fruit's bouquet.

Siren's Red Delight

Beneath the trees, a gleaming prize,
A tempting fruit that fills the skies.
Bright and round, it calls my name,
Do you dare to join the game?

Sipping cider, making bets,
Siren songs and no regrets.
With every crunch, the laughter flies,
Two friends spinning silly lies.

Mischief brews like bees in bloom,
We've turned the orchard into a room.
Dance like a fool, twirl like a breeze,
Juicy bites? Oh, if you please!

Tossing apples, playing catch,
Each red orb a perfect match.
Sticky cheeks and trailing laughs,
In our world, we're silly staff!

A Symphony of Rock and Fruit

From rocky trails to trees so grand,
We march together, hand in hand.
The melody of crunching cheer,
Happy tunes for all to hear.

Each step a joke, a skip, a giggle,
The ground beneath begins to wiggle.
An orchestra of fun unfolds,
As fruity tales delight retold.

With every swing, a note that's clear,
The laughter grows, we feel no fear.
A cannonball of fruit takes flight,
Splashing colors, pure delight!

Bouncing off the rocks, we play,
In nature's realm, a bright ballet.
Together, we compose the tune,
Underneath the sunny moon!

Serendipity in Every Crunch

In a world where fruits take flight,
Sweet surprises bring delight.
A stumble here, a tumble there,
Laughter echoes in the air.

What a time to skip and roll,
Silly giggles fill our soul.
Each crispy bite tells a tale,
Of adventures bold, without fail!

A picnic spreads beneath the trees,
Crunching joy flows like a breeze.
Unexpected wins at every turn,
For fruit, it seems, we all yearn.

With sticky hands, our hearts collide,
In every slice, new worlds abide.
Wanderlust fuels our playful munch,
Serendipity in every crunch!

Radiance in the Orchard

In the orchard bright and bold,
Laughter echoes, stories told.
Juicy treasure, round and sweet,
Beneath our feet, the laughter's heat.

Maggie's hat flew, caught a branch,
While Timmy tripped in his own dance.
Red ones rolling down the lane,
Who knew these fruits could drive us insane?

Squeezing juice, a sticky plight,
With beards of foam, what a sight!
Ducklings quack and join the fun,
As we giggle under the sun.

The harvest ends, but they're still there,
Piling up with flair and care.
Smiles and giggles, joy anew,
Just another day in our fruity zoo.

The Great Fruit Expedition

Off we go with bags in hand,
Waddling like a funny band.
Scavengers of tasty loot,
In search of nature's best fruit.

Bouncing berries, cherry pies,
Chasing dreams 'neath sunny skies.
Tommy trips and starts to roll,
His fruit-filled cap is on a pole!

A secret stash beneath a tree,
We find the curliest root, whee!
Amidst the laughs, we start to climb,
Each little step a silly rhyme.

At the top, what do we see?
An orchard grand, our jubilee!
With fruit hats worn like a crown,
We laugh until the world spins 'round.

Discoveries in Dappled Light

In dappled light, we roam so free,
Giggles lift like honeybee.
Fragrant wonders all around,
In this secret, playful ground.

Whispers float from tree to tree,
A fruity game for you and me.
We pluck and toss with gleeful cries,
While squirrels plot their own surprise.

Grapes in pockets, peaches shared,
Every bite makes us feel prepared.
Chasing shadows, making friends,
This jolly quest never ends.

As evening falls, the stars come out,
We dance and sing, there's never doubt.
In our hearts forever bright,
The magic lives in sweet delight.

The Dreamer's Orchard

In a dream, I found a place,
Where fruits and laughter interlace.
Skies are pink, and trees are tall,
I taste the juice, I feel the fall.

Chasing whimsy, up I climb,
Giggling at the silliest rhyme.
Sitting high, what a good view,
Watch the antics of the crew.

Clumsy critters, rolling round,
Chasing each other, noise profound.
With every snack, a burst of glee,
The joy of this odd jubilee.

When I awake, I'll hold it tight,
The dream of wonder, pure delight.
In the morning sun, I'll surely find,
The spirit of fun that's unconfined.

A Basket Full of Wonders

A basket filled with treasures bright,
Each fruit a giggle, pure delight.
Squeezed in tight, oh what a sight,
A race to munch from day to night.

The juiciest laughs take center stage,
As silly faces try to gauge.
Bites taken quick, they set the page,
Of summer tales that never age.

We tumble with glee, the paths do curl,
As sticky fingers make us twirl.
Chasing crumbs with a playful whirl,
Our laughter dances like a pearl.

So grab a fruit and join the spree,
For giggles grow on every tree.
In this fun ride, it's clear to see,
A basket full, just you and me.

Secrets of the Orchard Realm

In a land where the sun does shine,
We wander, twisting like a vine.
Every tree holds a joke divine,
Whispered winds, a fruity sign.

A branch will wave, a leaf will wink,
Come find the fun, don't stop to think.
With every bite, we share a link,
In laughter's joy, we all will sink.

From pies to cider, the magic brews,
Each tasty morsel brings us news.
With each new nibble, we can't refuse,
Our giggly hearts, a colorful fuse.

In this realm where wonders grow,
We skip and laugh, our spirits glow.
Each secret treasure we now sow,
Reveals the joy we've come to know.

The Road Beneath the Boughs

Winding paths below the trees,
Where playful whispers tease the breeze.
We dance in circles, laugh with ease,
In this hidden world, we aim to please.

Boughs hang low, a leafy dome,
We weave between, our merry home.
Like goofy sprites, we freely roam,
With fruity treats, we conquer foam.

Soon we discover a bumpy hill,
Rolling down, we've had our fill.
Each tumble ends with a hearty thrill,
As laughter echoes, time stands still.

With sticky hands and muddy knees,
We share sweet tales like honey bees.
Each step taken, our hearts appease,
On a road beneath the boughs, we seize.

Crate of Courage

A crate awaits with treasures rare,
Filled with flavors beyond compare.
To brave the munch with zest and flair,
In this silly game, do dare, do dare!

The first bite brings a hilarious surprise,
Squishy goodness, oh the cries!
As we munch, the laughter flies,
With every taste, we claim the skies.

With friends beside, we take our stand,
Tasting tales from far-off land.
In goofy bites, we make a brand,
Of silliness that's close at hand.

We dip and dive, the joy a whirl,
From fruity feasts, our giggles unfurl.
In this crate, our dreams unfurl,
With each new crunch, our hearts will twirl.

Chronicles of the Hidden Grove

In a grove where shadows play,
The fruit wears hats, come join the fray.
With squirrels dancing in the trees,
And laughter carried by the breeze.

A rabbit holds a secret map,
He swears it leads to treasure—snap!
With every step, the ground's alive,
Follow the giggles, let's all dive!

There's talk of a pie contest near,
But first, we must quell our fear.
Of sneaky raccoons dressed in style,
Who'll rob us blind with a slick smile!

At dusk, the magic starts to bloom,
As fireflies light up the gloom.
With friends so odd, let's take a stand,
And conquer this outlandish land!

The Call of the Orchard's Heart

A talking tree called out my name,
With branches waving like a game.
It said, 'Come closer, lend an ear,
I've tales of fruit that smell like beer!'

I tripped on roots that sang and danced,
In this wild place, I was entranced.
There's cider flowing from a brook,
With a recipe no one can cook!

I met a crow who lost a bet,
He wears a wig and can't forget.
'Join my crew,' he cawed with glee,
'There's mishaps waiting—just you see!'

Together we scoured hills of bliss,
Chasing giggles, not one to miss.
The orchard's heart beats ever loud,
In this wacky, whimsical crowd!

Secrets Ripe for Adventure

Underneath the leafy skies,
Lies a world of sweet surprise.
Bouncing berries wear mustaches,
They trip and giggle, one then crashes!

A fox with glasses reads the charts,
Mapping routes for daring hearts.
He claims he's found a hidden stash,
Of jellybeans that make you dash!

I joined a race, but oh, what fun,
As frogs in hats began to run.
They leapt and croaked, the ground could shake,
I laughed so hard, I thought I'd break!

The sun began to set with flair,
A golden glow in the cool air.
So many secrets yet to find,
In this land of the truly unrefined!

Enchanted Quest Amidst the Branches

With a map made of crumpled leaf,
My friends and I sought sweet relief.
We marched through thickets, wild and bright,
Chasing giggles, oh what a sight!

A parrot squawked a riddle loud,
While insects formed a dancing crowd.
'What weighs a pound, yet floats on air?'
We guessed, and guessed—our brains laid bare!

A trapdoor opened with a creak,
To find a feast was all we seeked.
With cupcakes topped with fruity eyes,
We munched and laughed beneath the skies!

So up we climbed to tree-top high,
With branches brushing 'gainst the sky.
In this enchanted, merry place,
Adventure finds us every space!

The Courageous Orchard Explorer

In a tree of dreams, I climbed so high,
A squirrel waved by, with a twinkle in eye.
I asked him the secrets of fruits in the air,
He chuckled and tossed me a golden pear.

With bucket in hand, I strolled through the green,
Where giggles of wind made the branches keen.
A ticket to fun, with each step anew,
But watch for the bees, they'll steal a bite too!

Under the shade, I found a surprise,
A picnic of colors, much to my eyes.
I danced with the shadows, a jester I'd be,
Till a pie-flying ghost said, "Come share with me!"

With friends made of fruit, I made quite a crew,
Together we sang, all my worries flew.
In the orchard of laughter, I'd found my new quest,
As the bravest explorer, I felt truly blessed.

Tasting the Rainbows

A fruit stand beacon, so bright and so bold,
With flavors like magic, and stories retold.
I took a small bite, and oh what delight,
The strawberry giggled, "Join in on this flight!"

Bananas were dreaming of castles in Spain,
While oranges waltzed with a splash of champagne.
Kiwi and mango marveled in glee,
In a carnival party hosted by me!

Jellybeans traded for whispers of bliss,
While cherries were plotting their next juicy kiss.
We painted the sky with the flavor parade,
And danced with the twilight till daylight displayed.

So if you should wander where colors collide,
Grab a spoon of joy, let your taste buds decide.
For each bite's an adventure, a laugh, and a cheer,
In the land of the rainbow, there's nothing to fear!

The Orchard's Hidden Paths

Down hidden lanes where the wild things play,
I spotted a path that had vanished away.
Whispers of fruit beckoned me near,
Telling of treasures that sparkled with cheer.

Through brambles and bushes, a challenge arose,
With hedgehogs and rabbits all wearing fine clothes.
"Join us for tea!" they all jumped and they cheered,
With scones made of sunshine, I gladly appeared.

A map drawn in berry juice showed the way,
To secrets unwrapped in a fruity ballet.
I stumbled on laughter, I leaped through a stream,
Finding treasures of fun in a whimsical dream.

As day turned to night, with the stars in full view,
The orchard was lively, as if it just knew.
With pies in the sky and a pizza-shaped moon,
I danced with the shadows to a comical tune!

In Pursuit of Juicy Legends

With pockets of wonders, I set off one morn,
To chase down the legends of orchards reborn.
The tales were so wild, with giggles galore,
Of fruit-throwing giants and sweet candy lore.

I found a sly fox in a hat made of gold,
Who whispered of secrets that never grew old.
"Follow the squawks of the mystical bird,
Where fruit grows in laughter, and humor is heard!"

Amidst rolling hills and a skip in my step,
I raced through the meadows where silly things crept.
With each silly stumble, more laughter would flow,
And the legends grew taller, like trees in a row.

So if you're seeking tales that are juicy and bright,
Look deep in the orchard, where dreams take their flight.
For legends abound if you dare take a peek,
In the kingdom of fruits, where smiles are unique!

www.ingramcontent.com/pod-product-compliance
Lightning Source LLC
Chambersburg PA
CBHW070323120526
44590CB00017B/2805